Living & Working Abroad
How to avoid getting into trouble with the IRS

Living & Working Abroad
How to avoid getting into trouble with the IRS

by
Claudia Moncarz

To Felippe, Sara and Samuel, you mean the world to me. Thank you for your constant support.

Table of Contents

Acknowledgement

Thank you to Jennifer Blanchard for been an amazing editor and pushing me to get this done. #Dreamlifeorbust

Thank you to Heidi Burgoyne for her amazing legal tax research skills. I am so proud of the amazing tax lawyer you are becoming.

Thank you to Jassen Bowman for all the support and clarity you have indirectly and directly provided.

Introduction

Hooray! You've been assigned to work abroad. I know how excited you are because I am a fellow travel junkie. (Actually, I'm a bit jealous that you're getting paid to live abroad.) You likely have the basic logistics covered: housing, work assignments, restaurants to eat at and places to explore, even side trips to take on the weekend. However, have you given some thought to taxes?

Don't give me that eyes-glazed look—taxes are something we all have to deal with. Luckily, you're reading this book, and you are in good hands, because I'm a certified tax geek. (I even teach this topic at law school.)

But I understand that you don't share my enthusiasm for tax. So I would like to give you the basics you will need to know, without putting you to sleep. This is a snooze-free zone. Are you ready?

This book will cover three basic areas[1]:

---

[1] Many cities and states in the United States levy a separate income or transfer tax systems on individuals. The residency rules in each state and city varied; it would be impossible to discuss each state's taxation law in this brief chapter.

1. Income tax and how to make sure you don't pay more than you should.

2. Capital gains.

3. Foreign reporting.

Let's start our adventure into the tax world.

Chapter 1

Income Tax

I know this will sound crazy, but unfortunately it's true, as a general rule, if you are a U.S. citizen or resident, your worldwide income and estate are subject to U.S. taxation. This rule applies regardless of where you are living and/or working in the world.

Yes, that's right, you are required to pay taxes on the income you make while working abroad. You will also be subject to the same income tax filing requirements that apply to citizens and residents living in the United States.

Let's talk a little more about each requirement:

A. **Filing Requirements**

The rules for filing tax returns and paying estimated tax are generally the same whether you're living in the United States or abroad. To determine if you need to file a tax return go to https://www.irs.gov/help/ita/do-i-need-to-file-a-tax-return   and follow the interactive quiz.

As a general rule, if you generated income above the threshold amounts you are required to file an income tax return (Form 1040: U.S. Individual Income Tax). This rule applies even if you may qualify for certain deductions, such as the Foreign Income Exclusion.

The definition of income includes all money you receive, regardless of the form. It could be cash, property, goods, services or benefits. This includes your base salary and bonuses, cost of living allowance, housing allowance, education allowance, home leave reimbursement, reimbursement of foreign taxes, personal use of a company car, certain moving allowances and stock options.

Basically, the definition of income covers everything unless you can find a specific exclusion in the tax code.

The deadline to file and pay your federal income taxes is April 15 of the following year. If you need additional time to file your return, you can request an automatic six-month extension. This is done by filing an Application for Automatic Extension of Time To File U.S. Individual Income Tax Return (Form 4868). In addition, you may get an extension to pay your taxes. While it is usually difficult to get an extension of time to pay, you can get an automatic two-month extension (i.e., until June 15) if you work and live abroad on the date your return is due (i.e., April 15). However, even if you get an extension to pay without any penalties, you will still have to pay interest on the amount owed.

In addition to the regular automatic six-month extension, U.S. citizens and residents living abroad can request an additional discretionary two-month extension of time (i.e. to December 15) to file their tax return. While this additional extension is discretionary, you will only receive correspondence from the IRS if your request has been denied.

You generally cannot get an extension of more than six months. However, if you are outside the United States and meet the requirements described below, you may be able to get a longer extension. You should consider requesting an extension if all three of the following apply:

1. You are a U.S. citizen or resident alien.

2. You expect to meet either the Bona Fide Residence test or the Physical Presence Test, but not until after your tax return is due. (The definitions for these two tests can be found in section D. Foreign Earned Income Exclusion.)

3. Your tax home is in a foreign country (or countries) throughout your period of bona fide residence or physical presence, whichever applies.

Self-Employed Tip:

If you are self-employed you must file an income tax return if you earn at least $400. This applies even if you netted less than that. Remember the IRS doesn't know what your deductions are.

ACTION STEPS:

1. Write down the deadline to file your federal income tax return. Now write down that date in your calendar.

2. Determine whether you will need to request an automatic extension. Some things to think about are:

    a. Do you have to file a tax return in the country you are living? If yes, have you already filed it?

    b. Do you meet the requirements to exclude your foreign earned income? If no, would you meet them if you filed your return at a later date?

    c. Do you have all the paperwork you will need to prepare the return?

    d. If you are using an accountant to prepare your tax return, is your accountant well versed in this area? Does your accountant have experience with international tax issues? Do you need more time to find one?

3. If you decided to request an extension, write down the deadline for filing an extension. Now write down that date in your calendar.

4. If you requested an automatic 6-month extension to file your tax return, write down your new filing date. Now write down that date in your calendar.

B. **Withholding Income Tax**

Your U.S. employer generally has a duty to withhold U.S. income taxes from your salary, even if you are working abroad. There are only two exemptions to this rule: if your employer reasonably believes you will exclude your income under the Foreign Earned Income Exclusion or the Foreign Housing Exclusion. (Don't worry, I will explain these two important exclusions later in the book. I promise.)

In order to fall under the second exemption, you would need to give your employer a statement indicating you expect to qualify for the Foreign Earned Income Exclusion under either the bona fide residence test or the physical presence test and indicating your estimated housing cost exclusion.

If you are a US citizen, you may use Form 673 (Statement for Claiming Exemption From Withholding on Foreign Earned Income Eligible for the Exclusion(s) Provided by Section 911) in lieu of a prepared statement.

C. **Withholding U.S. Social Security and Medicare Tax**

In general, U.S. social security and medicare taxes do not apply to wages for services you perform as an employee outside the United States unless one of the following exceptions applies:

1. You worked on or in connection with an American vessel or aircraft and you were either employed in the U.S. or the aircraft or vessel touches a U.S. port while you are employed. (This really only applies if you work on a ship or a plane registered in the US).

2. You are working in one of the countries with which the United States has entered into a bilateral social security agreement.

3. You are working for an American employer. This is the big catch-all section. According to US tax law, you work for an American employer if you work for:

    a. The U.S. Government or any of its agencies.

    b. An individual who is a resident of the United States.

c. A partnership of which at least two-thirds of the partners are U.S. residents.

d. A U.S. trust.

e. A U.S. corporation.

f. If you are performing services in connection with a contract between the U.S. government and a foreign person. I told you this was the catch-all section!

4. You are working for a foreign affiliate of an American employer who has entered into a voluntary agreement with the U.S. Treasury Department.

The one exemption to the above rule is when there is a Bilateral Social Security (Totalization) Agreement between the U.S. and a foreign country. What this basically means is that the United States has reached agreements with certain foreign countries to eliminate dual coverage and dual contributions (taxes) to social security systems for the same work. Once in a while the IRS tries to be fair. (I am serious, don't roll your eyes.)

Self-Employed Tip:

As a general rule, self-employed persons who are subject to dual taxation will only be covered by the social security system of the country where they reside. If your self-employment earnings should be exempt from foreign social security tax and subject only to U.S. self-employment tax, you should request a certificate of coverage from the U.S. Social Security Administration, Office of International Programs. The certificate will establish your exemption from the foreign social security tax.

ACTION STEPS:

1. Is your employer is required to withhold for U.S. social security taxes and Medicare? ___ yes___ no

2. If no, you are done, go to the next section.

3. If yes, determine if you you live in a country with a Bilateral Social Security (Totalization) Agreement with the US. ___ yes ___ no

4. If yes, then follow the rules in the Bilateral Social Security (Totalization) Agreement to avoid trouble taxation.

D. Foreign Earned Income Exclusion

As promised, let's talk about one of the most important concepts you need to learn about now that you are about to live and work abroad: the Foreign Earned Income Exclusion. As I already mentioned, if you are a U.S. citizen or resident and you live abroad, you are taxed on your worldwide income. However, if you meet certain requirements, you may qualify for the Foreign Earned Income Exclusion and Foreign Housing Exclusion/Deduction. These exclusions allow you to exclude from your taxable income up to $104,100 of your foreign earnings in 2018.

Self-Employed Tip:
When determining if you earned your income outside the U.S., the key is not where the money is coming from (i.e. in what country your client is paying you from) but where you did the work at.

To claim the Foreign Earned Income Exclusion or the Foreign Housing Exclusion/Deduction, you must meet all three of the following requirements:

1. Your tax home must be in a foreign country. By tax home, I mean your main place of business;

2. You must have earned the income outside the United States; and

3. You must either meet the bona fide resident or physical presence test. The requirements for these tests are as follows:

   a. Bona Fide Resident Test - A U.S. citizen or resident who is a bona fide resident of a foreign country or countries for an uninterrupted period that includes an entire tax year.

   b. Physical Presence Test - A U.S. citizen or a U.S. resident alien who is physically present in a foreign country or countries for at least 330 full days during any period of twelve consecutive months. For a day to be counted toward the 330 days, it must be a full 24-hour period beginning with midnight and ending with midnight.

If you qualify for this exclusion, you may also be able to exclude or deduct certain foreign housing amounts and the value of meals and lodging provided to you by your employer. However, there is a cap on the foreign housing expenses deduction.

If you qualify for these exclusions, you must make an election to have these amounts excluded from your income. The election is made with Form 2555: Foreign Earned Income, which is then attached to your federal income tax return (Form 1040).

ACTION STEPS:

1. Determine if you qualify for the foreign earned income exclusion. You must answer "yes" to the following three requirements.

    a. Is your main place of business in a foreign country? ___ yes ___ no

    b. Did you earn the income outside the United States? ___ yes ___ no

    c. Did you meet either meet the Bona Fide Resident or Physical Presence Test? ___ yes ___ no

2. Determine if you qualify for the foreign housing exclusion or the foreign housing deduction.

E. Foreign Tax Credit or Deduction

If you don't qualify for the foreign earned income and housing exclusion, you may be able to qualify for the foreign tax credit or deduction, U.S. citizens and residents are allowed either a deduction or credit against their U.S. income tax liability for income taxes paid or accrued during the tax year in any foreign country or U.S. possession. However, there is a limitation to this credit or deduction. The foreign tax credit or deduction is limited to the portion of the U.S. income tax liability that is related to foreign-source income.

In plain English, you can only take a foreign tax credit/deduction for income that is taxed both in the U.S. and the foreign country. Another limitation is that if you claimed either the Foreign Earned Income or Foreign Housing Exclusion, you cannot take a foreign tax credit against that excluded income. No double dipping.

Chapter 2

Capital Gains

The same rules that apply to U.S. citizens and residents living in the United States apply to those living abroad. Capital gains from the sale of investment assets held for less than twelve months are taxed at the taxpayer's regular tax rate. Sale of investment assets held for more than twelve months are generally taxed at the more favorable capital rate tax. So keep on reporting this income just as you did when you were living in the U.S. There is no major change in here.

Chapter 3

Foreign Assets Disclosure

Not only are U.S. citizens and residents taxed on their worldwide income, but they are also subject to strict reporting requirements on certain foreign assets. There are many reporting requirements related to foreign assets and transactions that you may be subject to, but for the purpose of this book we will discuss the two main ones: reporting foreign bank accounts and foreign financial assets.

A. Foreign Bank Accounts

If you have foreign bank accounts with an aggregate balance of $10,000 (or more) at any point in the calendar year, then you are required to report all your foreign bank accounts to the IRS. This disclosure is done in FinCEN Form 49342G. You will need to give the IRS information, such as your account number, name of your bank and your highest balance of the year. I want to make clear that this is just an information return as opposed to a tax return (in which you may have to pay taxes). You don't pay any taxes on this return, but the IRS does use the information from this return to make sure you are reporting all foreign source income (i.e. the interest generated in the account).

Originally, the disclosure was due in June of the following year, but starting in 2017, the disclosure is due at the same time as your income tax return.

Now we need to talk about when you're actually subject to this requirement.

First, let's talk about the $10,000 threshold. The key word here is *aggregate*. That means, for example, if you have ten accounts with a thousand dollars in each, then by aggregate you have $10,000 in foreign bank accounts, you have to report your foreign bank accounts to the IRS.

Let's say that you have two foreign bank accounts. Each account has as balance of $4,000 on January 1. Then in March you transfer $3,000 from Account One to Account Two. So now the balance in one account is $7,000 and the other is $1,000. Guess what? You are subject to this reporting requirement. Why, you ask? Because you have to look at the highest total balance throughout the year and add them together to see if that amount is over $10,000. In this example, at one point the highest balance in one account was $4,000 and the highest balance in another account was $7,000. And that adds up to $11,000, which is over the reporting amount. Yes, you are counting the amounts twice. Yes, it is crazy!

Another important thing to keep in mind is that this requirement applies to every account to which you are authorized signature (i.e. you can sign checks for the account) even if you are not the owner of the account. This is especially tricky when you are authorized to sign for your foreign company's account, but don't own the money in it. Your foreign company does not want to have to report their highest balance to the U.S. government. However, not reporting it is not an option. The penalties are too high: $10,000, at a minimum, or 50 percent of the highest balance, if the IRS finds out about the account before you disclose it. And trust me the IRS will find out about the account eventually. Nowadays, there is too much financial information sharing between the U.S. and other countries. And the EU is actually thinking of enacting similar laws because of the success the U.S. has had on the international tax front. So like Nancy Regan says: "Just Say No" to not reporting your foreign accounts.

As a final note, certain financial accounts such as pensions and mutual funds may be part of this disclosure requirement.

ACTION STEPS:

1. Make a list of all the foreign bank accounts and financial accounts that you were authorized to sign for last year.

2. Now determine the highest balance for each account last year.

3. Add up the highest balance for each of the foreign bank accounts.

4. If the total is equal to or greater than $10,000, you have to report your foreign bank accounts. If the total is less than $10,000, then no need to report your foreign bank accounts this year.

B. Foreign Assets

Around 2010, the IRS took foreign reporting a step further by requiring U.S. citizens and residents to report the financial assets they own worldwide, even if these assets do not generate any income or profits. Not only do you have to report when you receive certain gifts from a foreigner or if you have a foreign bank account, but now you also have to report when you have certain financial foreign assets. The failure to do so can be quite expensive: $10,000 for the first month, with a potential additional $10,000 for each 30-day period during which you continue to fail to file the information return. (Ouch!).

OK so now for the important question: do you have to worry about this?

The question of whether you are required to report your foreign financial assets is answered in four steps:

Step One: Determine whether you fall under the definition of "U.S. person."

If you picked up this book, I am going to assume you are a U.S. person, but nevertheless let's go over the definition. A U.S. person includes U.S. citizens, anyone who has a green card or anyone who meets the Substantial Presence Test (commonly referred to as the 183-Days Test). However, if you fall under the definition of U.S. person, that doesn't necessarily mean you have this reporting requirement.

Step Two: Determine whether you own "foreign financial assets."

A foreign financial assets is: foreign bank accounts; stocks or bonds from a foreign company; certain interests in a foreign estate or trust; foreign debt; ownership in a foreign company; and certain interests in a foreign pension plan.

Step Three: Determine whether the aggregate value of your foreign financial assets meets the reporting requirements threshold.

The reporting thresholds are below. Please note that you will need to have an idea of the value of each of the above-listed assets.

If you are single or married, but filing separately, you are required to report your foreign financial assets if the aggregate value exceeds: $200,000 on the last day of the tax year or exceeds $300,000 at any time during the tax year. The threshold amounts are double if you are married and filing jointly ($400,000 on the last day of the tax year or $600,000 at any time during the tax year).

Step Four: Determine whether you are required to file an annual return.

Unlike the foreign bank account reporting requirement, this reporting requirement only applies to those individuals who are required to file an information or income tax return (i.e. Forms 1040, 1040NR, 1120, 1065, 1041, and 1120-S). If you do not have to file an income tax return, you do not have to report your foreign financial assets, even if the value of your specified foreign financial assets is more than the reporting threshold.

ACTION STEPS:

1. Determine whether you fall under the definition of U.S. person.

2. Determine whether you own "foreign financial assets."

3. Determine whether the aggregate value of your foreign financial assets meets the reporting requirements thresholds.

4. Determine whether you are required to file an annual return.

Even though exciting adventures await you in your new life working abroad, you must carefully consider how your tax footprint abroad will impact your tax liability in the United States.

Bon Voyage!

FORM 1040

Form **1040** Department of the Treasury—Internal Revenue Service (99)
U.S. Individual Income Tax Return 2017 OMB No. 1545-0074 IRS Use Only—Do not write or staple in this space.

For the year Jan. 1–Dec. 31, 2017, or other tax year beginning , 2017, ending , 20   See separate instructions.

Your first name and initial	Last name	Your social security number

If a joint return, spouse's first name and initial	Last name	Spouse's social security number

Home address (number and street). If you have a P.O. box, see instructions.	Apt. no.	▲ Make sure the SSN(s) above and on line 6c are correct.

City, town or post office, state, and ZIP code. If you have a foreign address, also complete spaces below (see instructions).

Presidential Election Campaign
Check here if you, or your spouse if filing jointly, want $3 to go to this fund. Checking a box below will not change your tax or refund. ☐ You ☐ Spouse

Foreign country name	Foreign province/state/county	Foreign postal code

Filing Status

Check only one box.

1 ☐ Single
2 ☐ Married filing jointly (even if only one had income)
3 ☐ Married filing separately. Enter spouse's SSN above and full name here. ▶
4 ☐ Head of household (with qualifying person). (See instructions.) If the qualifying person is a child but not your dependent, enter this child's name here. ▶
5 ☐ Qualifying widow(er) (see instructions)

Exemptions

6a ☐ Yourself. If someone can claim you as a dependent, **do not** check box 6a . . . . . ▶
b ☐ Spouse . . . .

c Dependents:		(2) Dependent's social security number	(3) Dependent's relationship to you	(4) ✓ if child under age 17 qualifying for child tax credit (see instructions)
(1) First name	Last name			
				☐
				☐
				☐
				☐

If more than four dependents, see instructions and check here ▶ ☐

d Total number of exemptions claimed . . . .

Boxes checked on 6a and 6b
No. of children on 6c who:
• lived with you
• did not live with you due to divorce or separation (see instructions)
Dependents on 6c not entered above
Add numbers on lines above ▶

Income

Attach Form(s) W-2 here. Also attach Forms W-2G and 1099-R if tax was withheld.

If you did not get a W-2, see instructions.

7 Wages, salaries, tips, etc. Attach Form(s) W-2 7
8a Taxable interest. Attach Schedule B if required 8a
b Tax-exempt interest. **Do not** include on line 8a . . . 8b
9a Ordinary dividends. Attach Schedule B if required 9a
b Qualified dividends 9b
10 Taxable refunds, credits, or offsets of state and local income taxes 10
11 Alimony received 11
12 Business income or (loss). Attach Schedule C or C-EZ 12
13 Capital gain or (loss). Attach Schedule D if required. If not required, check here ▶ ☐ 13
14 Other gains or (losses). Attach Form 4797 14
15a IRA distributions . 15a b Taxable amount . . . 15b
16a Pensions and annuities 16a b Taxable amount . . . 16b
17 Rental real estate, royalties, partnerships, S corporations, trusts, etc. Attach Schedule E 17
18 Farm income or (loss). Attach Schedule F 18
19 Unemployment compensation 19
20a Social security benefits 20a b Taxable amount . . . 20b
21 Other income. List type and amount _____ 21
22 Combine the amounts in the far right column for lines 7 through 21. This is your **total income** ▶ 22

Adjusted Gross Income

23 Educator expenses 23
24 Certain business expenses of reservists, performing artists, and fee-basis government officials. Attach Form 2106 or 2106-EZ 24
25 Health savings account deduction. Attach Form 8889 . 25
26 Moving expenses. Attach Form 3903 26
27 Deductible part of self-employment tax. Attach Schedule SE . 27
28 Self-employed SEP, SIMPLE, and qualified plans . . 28
29 Self-employed health insurance deduction 29
30 Penalty on early withdrawal of savings 30
31a Alimony paid b Recipient's SSN ▶ 31a
32 IRA deduction 32
33 Student loan interest deduction 33
34 Tuition and fees. Attach Form 8917 34
35 Domestic production activities deduction. Attach Form 8903 35
36 Add lines 23 through 35 36
37 Subtract line 36 from line 22. This is your **adjusted gross income** . . . . . ▶ 37

For Disclosure, Privacy Act, and Paperwork Reduction Act Notice, see separate instructions. Cat. No. 11320B Form **1040** (2017)

Tax and Credits	38	Amount from line 37 (adjusted gross income)	38
	39a	Check if: ☐ **You** were born before January 2, 1953, ☐ Blind. **Total boxes** ☐ **Spouse** was born before January 2, 1953, ☐ Blind. checked ▶ 39a	
	b	If your spouse itemizes on a separate return or you were a dual-status alien, check here▶ 39b☐	
Standard Deduction for— • People who check any box on line 39a or 39b **or** who can be claimed as a dependent, see instructions. • All others: Single or Married filing separately, $6,350 Married filing jointly or Qualifying widow(er), $12,700 Head of household, $9,350	40	**Itemized deductions** (from Schedule A) or your **standard deduction** (see left margin) . .	40
	41	Subtract line 40 from line 38	41
	42	**Exemptions.** If line 38 is $156,900 or less, multiply $4,050 by the number on line 6d. Otherwise, see instructions	42
	43	**Taxable income.** Subtract line 42 from line 41. If line 42 is more than line 41, enter -0- . .	43
	44	**Tax** (see instructions). Check if any from: **a** ☐ Form(s) 8814 **b** ☐ Form 4972 **c** ☐	44
	45	**Alternative minimum tax** (see instructions). Attach Form 6251	45
	46	Excess advance premium tax credit repayment. Attach Form 8962	46
	47	Add lines 44, 45, and 46 . . . . ▶	47
	48	Foreign tax credit. Attach Form 1116 if required	48	
	49	Credit for child and dependent care expenses. Attach Form 2441	49	
	50	Education credits from Form 8863, line 19	50	
	51	Retirement savings contributions credit. Attach Form 8880	51	
	52	Child tax credit. Attach Schedule 8812, if required . . .	52	
	53	Residential energy credits. Attach Form 5695	53	
	54	Other credits from Form: **a** ☐ 3800 **b** ☐ 8801 **c** ☐	54	
	55	Add lines 48 through 54. These are your **total credits** . . . . ▶	55
	56	Subtract line 55 from line 47. If line 55 is more than line 47, enter -0- . . . . . . ▶	56
Other Taxes	57	Self-employment tax. Attach Schedule SE	57
	58	Unreported social security and Medicare tax from Form: **a** ☐ 4137 **b** ☐ 8919	58
	59	Additional tax on IRAs, other qualified retirement plans, etc. Attach Form 5329 if required . .	59
	60a	Household employment taxes from Schedule H	60a
	b	First-time homebuyer credit repayment. Attach Form 5405 if required	60b
	61	Health care: individual responsibility (see instructions) Full-year coverage ☐	61
	62	Taxes from: **a** ☐ Form 8959 **b** ☐ Form 8960 **c** ☐ Instructions: enter code(s)	62
	63	Add lines 56 through 62. This is your **total tax** . . . . ▶	63
Payments If you have a qualifying child, attach Schedule EIC.	64	Federal income tax withheld from Forms W-2 and 1099	64	
	65	2017 estimated tax payments and amount applied from 2016 return	65	
	66a	**Earned income credit (EIC)**	66a	
	b	Nontaxable combat pay election	66b		
	67	Additional child tax credit. Attach Schedule 8812 . . .	67	
	68	American opportunity credit from Form 8863, line 8 . . .	68	
	69	Net premium tax credit. Attach Form 8962	69	
	70	Amount paid with request for extension to file	70	
	71	Excess social security and tier 1 RRTA tax withheld . . .	71	
	72	Credit for federal tax on fuels. Attach Form 4136	72	
	73	Credits from Form: **a** ☐ 2439 **b** ☐ Reserved **c** ☐ 8885 **d** ☐	73	
	74	Add lines 64, 65, 66a, and 67 through 73. These are your **total payments** . . . . . ▶	74
Refund Direct deposit? See instructions.	75	If line 74 is more than line 63, subtract line 63 from line 74. This is the amount you **overpaid**	75
	76a	Amount of line 75 you want **refunded to you.** If Form 8888 is attached, check here . . ▶ ☐	76a
	▶ b	Routing number ▶ c Type: ☐ Checking ☐ Savings	
	▶ d	Account number	
	77	Amount of line 75 you want **applied to your 2018 estimated tax** ▶	77	
Amount You Owe	78	**Amount you owe.** Subtract line 74 from line 63. For details on how to pay, see instructions ▶	78
	79	Estimated tax penalty (see instructions)	79	

Third Party Designee

Do you want to allow another person to discuss this return with the IRS (see instructions)? ☐ **Yes. Complete below.** ☐ **No**

Designee's name ▶   Phone no. ▶   Personal identification number (PIN) ▶

Sign Here
Joint return? See instructions.
Keep a copy for your records.

Under penalties of perjury, I declare that I have examined this return and accompanying schedules and statements, and to the best of my knowledge and belief, they are true, correct, and accurately list all amounts and sources of income I received during the tax year. Declaration of preparer (other than taxpayer) is based on all information of which preparer has any knowledge.

Your signature   Date   Your occupation   Daytime phone number

Spouse's signature. If a joint return, **both** must sign.   Date   Spouse's occupation   If the IRS sent you an Identity Protection PIN, enter it here (see inst.)

Paid Preparer Use Only

Print/Type preparer's name   Preparer's signature   Date   Check ☐ if self-employed   PTIN

Firm's name ▶   Firm's EIN ▶

Firm's address ▶   Phone no.

FORM 4868

Form **4868**
(Rev. November 2017)
Department of the Treasury
Internal Revenue Service (99)

Application for Automatic Extension of Time To File U.S. Individual Income Tax Return

▶ Go to *www.irs.gov/Form4868* for the latest information.

OMB No. 1545-0074

2017

There are three ways to request an automatic extension of time to file a U.S. individual income tax return.

1. You can pay all or part of your estimated income tax due and indicate that the payment is for an extension using Direct Pay, the Electronic Federal Tax Payment System, or using a credit or debit card. See *How To Make a Payment*, on page 3.

2. You can file Form 4868 electronically by accessing IRS *e-file* using your home computer or by using a tax professional who uses *e-file*.

3. You can file a paper Form 4868 and enclose payment of your estimate of tax due.

It's Convenient, Safe, and Secure

IRS *e-file* is the IRS's electronic filing program. You can get an automatic extension of time to file your tax return by filing Form 4868 electronically. You'll receive an electronic acknowledgment once you complete the transaction. Keep it with your records. Don't mail in Form 4868 if you file electronically, unless you're making a payment with a check or money order (see page 3).

Complete Form 4868 to use as a worksheet. If you think you may owe tax when you file your return, you'll need to estimate your total tax liability and subtract how much you've already paid (lines 4, 5, and 6 below).

Several companies offer free e-filing of Form 4868 through the Free File program. For more details, go to IRS.gov and click on *freefile*.

Pay Electronically

You **don't** need to file Form 4868 if you make a payment using our electronic payment options. The IRS will automatically process an extension of time to file when you pay part or all of your estimated income tax electronically. You can pay online or by phone (see page 3).

E-file Using Your Personal Computer or Through a Tax Professional

Refer to your tax software package or tax preparer for ways to file electronically. Be sure to have a copy of your 2016 tax return— you'll be asked to provide information from the return for taxpayer verification. If you wish to make a payment, you can pay by electronic funds withdrawal or send your check or money order to the address shown in the middle column under *Where To File a Paper Form 4868* (see page 4).

File a Paper Form 4868

If you wish to file on paper instead of electronically, fill in the Form 4868 below and mail it to the address shown on page 4.

For information on using a private delivery service, see page 4.

Note: If you're a fiscal year taxpayer, you must file a paper Form 4868.

General Instructions

Purpose of Form

Use Form 4868 to apply for 6 more months (4 if "out of the country" (defined on page 2) and a U.S. citizen or resident) to file Form 1040, 1040A, 1040EZ, 1040NR, 1040NR-EZ, 1040-PR, or 1040-SS.

Gift and generation-skipping transfer (GST) tax return (Form 709). An extension of time to file your 2017 calendar year income tax return also extends the time to file Form 709 for 2017. However, it doesn't extend the time to pay any gift and GST tax you may owe for 2017. To make a payment of gift and GST tax, see Form 8892. If you don't pay the amount due by the regular due date for Form 709, you'll owe interest and may also be charged penalties. If the donor died during 2017, see the instructions for Forms 709 and 8892.

Qualifying for the Extension

To get the extra time you must:

1. Properly estimate your 2017 tax liability using the information available to you.

2. Enter your total tax liability on line 4 of Form 4868, and

3. File Form 4868 by the regular due date of your return.

 Although you aren't required to make a payment of the tax you estimate as due, Form 4868 doesn't extend the time to pay taxes. If you don't pay the amount due by the regular due date, you'll owe interest. You may also be charged penalties. For more details, see Interest and Late Payment Penalty on page 2. Any remittance you make with your application for extension will be treated as a payment of tax.

You don't have to explain why you're asking for the extension. We'll contact you only if your request is denied.

Don't file Form 4868 if you want the IRS to figure your tax or you're under a court order to file your return by the regular due date.

▼ DETACH HERE ▼

Form **4868**
(Rev. November 2017)
Department of the Treasury
Internal Revenue Service (99)

Application for Automatic Extension of Time To File U.S. Individual Income Tax Return

OMB No. 1545-0074

2017

For calendar year 2017, or other tax year beginning _____ , 2017, ending _____ , 20 ___

Part I Identification				**Part II** Individual Income Tax	
1 Your name(s) (see instructions)				4 Estimate of total tax liability for 2017 . .	$
				5 Total 2017 payments	
Address (see instructions)				6 **Balance due.** Subtract line 5 from line 4 (see instructions)	
				7 Amount you're paying (see instructions) . ▶	
City, town, or post office	State	ZIP Code		8 Check here if you're "out of the country" and a U.S. citizen or resident (see instructions) . . . . ▶ ☐	
2 Your social security number	3 Spouse's social security number			9 Check here if you file Form 1040NR or 1040NR-EZ and didn't receive wages as an employee subject to U.S. income tax withholding. . . . . ▶ ☐	

For Privacy Act and Paperwork Reduction Act Notice, see page 4.   Cat. No. 13141W   Form **4868** (2017) (Rev. 11-2017)

FORM 673

Form **673**
(Rev. December 2007)
Department of the Treasury
Internal Revenue Service

Statement for Claiming Exemption From Withholding on Foreign Earned Income Eligible for the Exclusion(s) Provided by Section 911

OMB No. 1545-0074

The following statement, when completed and furnished by a citizen of the United States to his or her employer, permits the employer to exclude from income tax withholding all or a part of the wages paid for services performed outside the United States.

Name (please print or type)	Social security number

Part I — Qualification Information for Foreign Earned Income Exclusion

I expect to qualify for the foreign earned income exclusion under either the bona fide residence or physical presence test for calendar year _____ or other tax year beginning _____ and ending _____ .

Please check applicable box:

☐ **Bona Fide Residence Test**

I am a citizen of the United States. I have been a bona fide resident of and my tax home has been located in
_____ (foreign country or countries) for an uninterrupted period which includes an entire tax year that began on _____ , 20 _____ .

(date)

I expect to remain a bona fide resident and retain my tax home in a foreign country (or countries) until the end of the tax year for which this statement is made. Or, if not that period, from the date of this statement until
_____ , 20 _____ .
(date within tax year)

I have not submitted a statement to the authorities of any foreign country named above that I am not a resident of that country. Or, if I made such a statement, the authorities of that country thereafter made a determination to the effect that I am a resident of that country.

Based on the facts in my case, I have good reason to believe that for this period of foreign residence I will satisfy the tax home and the bona fide foreign resident requirements prescribed by section 911(d)(1)(A) of the Internal Revenue Code and qualify for the exclusion Code section 911(a) allows.

☐ **Physical Presence Test**

I am a citizen of the United States. Except for occasional absences that will not disqualify me for the benefit of section 911(a) of the Internal Revenue Code, I expect to be present in and maintain my tax home in
_____ (foreign country or countries) for a 12-month period that includes the entire tax year _____ . Or, if not the entire year, for the part of the tax year beginning on _____ , 20 _____ , and ending on _____ , 20 _____ .

Based on the facts in my case, I have good reason to believe that for this period of presence in a foreign country or countries, I will satisfy the tax home and the 330 full-day requirements within a 12-month period under section 911(d)(1)(B).

Part II — Estimated Housing Cost Amount for Foreign Housing Exclusion (see instructions)

1	Rent .	1	
2	Utilities (other than telephone charges)	2	
3	Real and personal property insurance .	3	
4	Occupancy tax not deductible under section 164 .	4	
5	Nonrefundable fees paid for securing a leasehold	5	
6	Household repairs	6	
7	**Estimated qualified housing expenses.** Add lines 1 through 6 .	7	
8	Estimated base housing amount for qualifying period	8	
9	Subtract line 8 from line 7. This is your estimated housing cost amount .	9	

Part III — Certification

Under penalties of perjury, I declare that I have examined the information on this form and to the best of my knowledge and belief it is true, correct, and complete. I further certify under penalties of perjury that:

● The estimated housing cost amount entered in Part II, plus the amount reported on any other statements outstanding with other employers, is not more than my total estimated housing cost amount.

● If I become disqualified for the exclusions, I will immediately notify my employer and advise what part, if any, of the period for which I am qualified.

I understand that any exemption from income tax withholding permitted by reason of furnishing this statement is not a determination by the Internal Revenue Service that any amount paid to me for any services performed during the tax year is excludable from gross income under the provisions of Code section 911(a).

Your Signature	Date

For Paperwork Reduction Act Notice, see back of form.   Cat. No. 10183Y   Form **673** (Rev. 12-2007)

FORM 2555

Form **2555**

Department of the Treasury
Internal Revenue Service

Foreign Earned Income

▶ Attach to Form 1040. Complete the Foreign Earned Income Tax Worksheet in the Instructions for Form 1040 if you enter an amount on lines 45 or 50.
▶ Go to *www.irs.gov/Form2555* for instructions and the latest information.

OMB No. 1545-0074

20**17**

Attachment
Sequence No. **34**

For Use by U.S. Citizens and Resident Aliens Only

Name shown on Form 1040

Your social security number

Part I   General Information

1   Your foreign address (including country)

2   Your occupation

3   Employer's name ▶

4a   Employer's U.S. address ▶

  b   Employer's foreign address ▶

5   Employer is (check any that apply):   **a** ☐ A foreign entity   **b** ☐ A U.S. company   **c** ☐ Self
     d ☐ A foreign affiliate of a U.S. company   **e** ☐ Other (specify) ▶

6a   If you previously filed Form 2555 or Form 2555-EZ, enter the last year you filed the form. ▶

  b   If you didn't previously file Form 2555 or 2555-EZ to claim either of the exclusions, check here ▶ ☐ and go to line 7.

  c   Have you ever revoked either of the exclusions? . . . . ☐ Yes ☐ No

  d   If you answered "Yes," enter the type of exclusion and the tax year for which the revocation was effective. ▶

7   Of what country are you a citizen/national? ▶

8a   Did you maintain a separate foreign residence for your family because of adverse living conditions at your tax home? See **Second foreign household** in the instructions . . . . ☐ Yes ☐ No

  b   If "Yes," enter city and country of the separate foreign residence. Also, enter the number of days during your tax year that you maintained a second household at that address. ▶

9   List your tax home(s) during your tax year and date(s) established. ▶

Next, complete either Part II or Part III. If an item doesn't apply, enter "NA." If you don't give the information asked for, any exclusion or deduction you claim may be disallowed.

Part II   Taxpayers Qualifying Under Bona Fide Residence Test (see instructions)

10   Date bona fide residence began ▶   , and ended ▶

11   Kind of living quarters in foreign country ▶   **a** ☐ Purchased house   **b** ☐ Rented house or apartment   **c** ☐ Rented room
     d ☐ Quarters furnished by employer

12a   Did any of your family live with you abroad during any part of the tax year? . . . . ☐ Yes ☐ No

  b   If "Yes," who and for what period? ▶

13a   Have you submitted a statement to the authorities of the foreign country where you claim bona fide residence that you aren't a resident of that country? See instructions . . . . ☐ Yes ☐ No

  b   Are you required to pay income tax to the country where you claim bona fide residence? See instructions . ☐ Yes ☐ No

     If you answered "Yes" to 13a and "No" to 13b, you don't qualify as a bona fide resident. Don't complete the rest of this part.

14   If you were present in the United States or its possessions during the tax year, complete columns **(a)–(d)** below. **Don't** include the income from column **(d)** in Part IV, but report it on Form 1040.

(a) Date arrived in U.S.	(b) Date left U.S.	(c) Number of days in U.S. on business	(d) Income earned in U.S. on business (attach computation)	(a) Date arrived in U.S.	(b) Date left U.S.	(c) Number of days in U.S. on business	(d) Income earned in U.S. on business (attach computation)

15a   List any contractual terms or other conditions relating to the length of your employment abroad. ▶

  b   Enter the type of visa under which you entered the foreign country. ▶

  c   Did your visa limit the length of your stay or employment in a foreign country? If "Yes," attach explanation . ☐ Yes ☐ No

  d   Did you maintain a home in the United States while living abroad? . . . . ☐ Yes ☐ No

  e   If "Yes," enter address of your home, whether it was rented, the names of the occupants, and their relationship to you. ▶

| **Part III** | **Taxpayers Qualifying Under Physical Presence Test** (see instructions) |

16 The physical presence test is based on the 12-month period from ▶ .... through ▶ ....

17 Enter your principal country of employment during your tax year. ▶ ....

18 If you traveled abroad during the 12-month period entered on line 16, complete columns **(a)–(f)** below. Exclude travel between foreign countries that didn't involve travel on or over international waters, or in or over the United States, for 24 hours or more. If you have no travel to report during the period, enter "Physically present in a foreign country or countries for the entire 12-month period." **Don't** include the income from column **(f)** below in Part IV, but report it on Form 1040.

(a) Name of country (including U.S.)	**(b)** Date arrived	**(c)** Date left	**(d)** Full days present in country	**(e)** Number of days in U.S. on business	**(f)** Income earned in U.S. on business (attach computation)

| **Part IV** | **All Taxpayers** |

Note: Enter on lines 19 through 23 all income, including noncash income, you earned and actually or constructively received during your 2017 tax year for services you performed in a foreign country. If any of the foreign earned income received this tax year was earned in a prior tax year, or will be earned in a later tax year (such as a bonus), see the instructions. **Don't** include income from line 14, column **(d)**, or line 18, column **(f)**. Report amounts in U.S. dollars, using the exchange rates in effect when you actually or constructively received the income.

If you are a cash basis taxpayer, report on Form 1040 all income you received in 2017, no matter when you performed the service.

2017 Foreign Earned Income		Amount (in U.S. dollars)
19	Total wages, salaries, bonuses, commissions, etc.	**19**	
20	Allowable share of income for personal services performed (see instructions):		
a	In a business (including farming) or profession	**20a**	
b	In a partnership. List partnership's name and address and type of income. ▶		
		20b	
21	Noncash income (market value of property or facilities furnished by employer—attach statement showing how it was determined):		
a	Home (lodging)	**21a**	
b	Meals	**21b**	
c	Car	**21c**	
d	Other property or facilities. List type and amount. ▶		
		21d	
22	Allowances, reimbursements, or expenses paid on your behalf for services you performed:		
a	Cost of living and overseas differential	**22a**		
b	Family	**22b**		
c	Education	**22c**		
d	Home leave	**22d**		
e	Quarters	**22e**		
f	For any other purpose. List type and amount. ▶			
		22f		
g	Add lines 22a through 22f	**22g**	
23	Other foreign earned income. List type and amount. ▶		
		23	
24	Add lines 19 through 21d, line 22g, and line 23	**24**	
25	Total amount of meals and lodging included on line 24 that is excludable (see instructions) . .	**25**	
26	Subtract line 25 from line 24. Enter the result here and on line 27 on page 3. This is your **2017 foreign earned income** . . . . ▶	**26**	

| **Part V** | All Taxpayers |

| 27 | Enter the amount from line 26 . . . . | 27 | |

Are you claiming the housing exclusion or housing deduction?
☐ **Yes.** Complete Part VI.
☐ **No.** Go to Part VII.

| **Part VI** | Taxpayers Claiming the Housing Exclusion and/or Deduction |

28	Qualified housing expenses for the tax year (see instructions)	28	
29a	Enter location where housing expenses incurred (see instructions) ▶		
b	Enter limit on housing expenses (see instructions)	29b	
30	Enter the **smaller** of line 28 or line 29b	30	
31	Number of days in your qualifying period that fall within your 2017 tax year (see instructions)	**31**	**days**		
32	Multiply $44.76 by the number of days on line 31. If 365 is entered on line 31, enter $16,336 here	32	
33	Subtract line 32 from line 30. If the result is zero or less, don't complete the rest of this part or any of Part IX	33	
34	Enter employer-provided amounts (see instructions)	**34**		
35	Divide line 34 by line 27. Enter the result as a decimal (rounded to at least three places), but don't enter more than "1.000"	35	× .
36	**Housing exclusion.** Multiply line 33 by line 35. Enter the result but don't enter more than the amount on line 34. Also, complete Part VIII . . . . ▶	36	

Note: The housing deduction is figured in Part IX. If you choose to claim the foreign earned income exclusion, complete Parts VII and VIII before Part IX.

| **Part VII** | Taxpayers Claiming the Foreign Earned Income Exclusion |

37	Maximum foreign earned income exclusion	37	$102,100 00
38	• If you completed Part VI, enter the number from line 31.			
	• All others, enter the number of days in your qualifying period that fall within your 2017 tax year (see the instructions for line 31). }	**38**	**days**	
39	• If line 38 and the number of days in your 2017 tax year (usually 365) are the same, enter "1.000."			
	• Otherwise, divide line 38 by the number of days in your 2017 tax year and enter the result as a decimal (rounded to at least three places). }	39	× .
40	Multiply line 37 by line 39	40	
41	Subtract line 36 from line 27	41	
42	**Foreign earned income exclusion.** Enter the **smaller** of line 40 or line 41. Also, complete Part VIII ▶	42	

| **Part VIII** | Taxpayers Claiming the Housing Exclusion, Foreign Earned Income Exclusion, or Both |

43	Add lines 36 and 42	43	
44	Deductions allowed in figuring your adjusted gross income (Form 1040, line 37) that are allocable to the excluded income. See instructions and attach computation	44	
45	Subtract line 44 from line 43. Enter the result here and in parentheses on **Form 1040, line 21.** Next to the amount enter "Form 2555." On Form 1040, subtract this amount from your income to arrive at total income on Form 1040, line 22	45	

| **Part IX** | Taxpayers Claiming the Housing Deduction—Complete this part only if **(a)** line 33 is more than line 36 and **(b)** line 27 is more than line 43. |

46	Subtract line 36 from line 33	46	
47	Subtract line 43 from line 27	47	
48	Enter the **smaller** of line 46 or line 47	48	

Note: If line 47 is **more than** line 48 and you couldn't deduct all of your 2016 housing deduction because of the 2016 limit, use the housing deduction carryover worksheet in the instructions to figure the amount to enter on line 49. Otherwise, go to line 50.

| 49 | Housing deduction carryover from 2016 (from the housing deduction carryover worksheet in the instructions) . . . . | 49 | |
| 50 | **Housing deduction.** Add lines 48 and 49. Enter the total here and on Form 1040 to the left of line 36. Next to the amount on Form 1040, enter "Form 2555." Add it to the total adjustments reported on that line . . . . ▶ | 50 | |

MEET CLAUDIA

Thank you for reading this book. I hope it will help you in our new journey. Now let me take this last couple of pages to introduce myself.

I am a world traveler, mother, number lover, and a great attorney (not to toot my own horn). While admittedly I am not that humble, I am proud to be a caring friend to my clients.

MY GLOBAL IDENTITY: IT'S IN THE GENES

I was born in Panama City, Panama but my family was not the kind to remain in one country for too long. There was too much of the world to explore. By age eight I had already lived in Panama, Mexico, and the United States. As an adult, I've visited numerous countries throughout Europe, South America, and Asia including China, Kuala Lumpur, Vietnam and still counting.

MY LOVE OF NUMBERS: IT'S ALSO IN THE GENES

Even though a love of numbers runs in my family (my grandparents were accountants), I had always shied away from a career related in any way to finance. In fact, my undergraduate major was in English literature. That changed once I got to law school. One summer, I landed an internship working for a criminal judge in Miami, Florida. He quickly realized that I did not want to practice criminal law, so he sent me to different divisions to observe other judges.

The week I spent in probate court changed my life. I finally learned what I wanted to do with the rest of my professional life: I was going to be a probate lawyer.

That fall, I shared my new plan with one of my professors. He advised I take a tax course, a recommendation that I reluctantly followed. Thank goodness I did. Studying tax law was like being in nirvana. My love affair with tax law began from that moment. I guess it was meant to be. After all, it is in genes.

www.ingramcontent.com/pod-product-compliance
Lightning Source LLC
Chambersburg PA
CBHW051335220526
45468CB00004B/1655